DEBORAH BRUCE

Deborah Bruce is a playwright and theatre director. Her other plays include *Godchild* at Hampstead Theatre, *Same* for the National Theatre Connections Festival 2014, *The Distance* at the Orange Tree Theatre and Sheffield Crucible, *The House They Grew Up In* at Chichester Festival Theatre, *Joanne* for Clean Break at Soho Theatre, *Guidesky and I* at the Orange Tree Theatre and *Raya* at Hampstead Theatre Downstairs. *The Distance* was a finalist for the 2012-13 Susan Smith Blackburn Prize.

Deborah Bruce

DIXON AND DAUGHTERS

NICK HERN BOOKS
London
www.nickhernbooks.co.uk

A Nick Hern Book

Dixon and Daughters first published in Great Britain in 2023 as a paperback original by Nick Hern Books Limited, The Glasshouse, 49a Goldhawk Road, London W12 8QP

Dixon and Daughters copyright © 2023 Deborah Bruce

Deborah Bruce has asserted her right to be identified as the author of this work

Cover image: Photography (Alison Fitzjohn, Andrea Lowe, Liz White) by Joné Reed

Designed and typeset by Nick Hern Books, London
Printed in Great Britain by Mimeo Ltd, Huntingdon, Cambridgeshire PE29 6XX

A CIP catalogue record for this book is available from the British Library

ISBN 978 1 83904 151 8

Dixon and Daughters was first performed in the Dorfman auditorium of the National Theatre, London, on 25 April 2023 (previews from 15 April). The cast was as follows:

MARY	Bríd Brennan
BRIANA	Alison Fitzjohn
ELLA	Yazmin Kayani
JULIE	Andrea Lowe
LEIGH	Posy Sterling
BERNIE	Liz White

Director	Róisín McBrinn
Set and Costume Designer	Kat Heath
Lighting Designer	Paule Constable
Sound Designer	Sinéad Diskin
Movement Director	Sarita Piotrowski
Fight Director	Bethan Clark
Casting	Bryony Jarvis-Taylor
Dialect Coach	Michaela Kennen
Company Voice Work	Shereen Ibrahim
Wellbeing Practitioner	Samantha Llewellyn
Associate Lighting Designer	Mildred Moyo
Staff Director	Monaé Robinson

Acknowledgements

I'd like to thank

Clare Barstow

Nina Steiger and Rufus Norris

Everyone at Clean Break especially Anna Hermann, Maya Ellis and Lorraine Maher

Giles Smart

Róisín McBrinn

Big thanks to Posy Sterling

Love and thanks to Jeremy, Barney and Nell Herrin

D.B.

To the Members of the Clean Break Writers Circle.

*With my thanks to each and every one of you for your
wholehearted generosity and inspiration.
You have changed the way I write.*

Characters

MARY, *sixty-four, widow of Ray Dixon*
BERNIE, *forty-one, daughter of Mary and Ray Dixon*
JULIE, *forty-three, daughter of Mary and Ray Dixon*
ELLA, *twenty-one, daughter of Bernie*
BRIANA, *forty-six, daughter of Ray Dixon*
LEIGH, *mid-twenties*

Note on Text

A forward slash (/) within a line indicates an interruption.
A forward slash at the end of a line means the next person
comes in straight away. A forward slash at the beginning of
a line means that the next line is spoken at the same time as
that line.

Note on Play

The play is set in a whole house comprising of a front room,
a kitchen, two bedrooms, a staircase and a hallway with
a front door.

This can be presented in a naturalistic or unnaturalistic way.

Action often takes place in more than one room at a time. The
dialogue in the play are the only words the characters speak, as
in, there is no mimed conversation while a scene is taking place
in another room.

The play should run straight through with no interval.

*This text went to press before the end of rehearsals and so may
differ slightly from the play as performed.*

1.

Lights up on a modest house in Bradford – maybe like a doll's house with the back taken off.

The house is still and empty, and tidy.

The front door opens, MARY enters with BERNIE.

BERNIE. In you come.

MARY *has a quick glance around before going straight into the downstairs toilet.*

BERNIE *goes into the sitting room.*

You hiding, because I wouldn't bother.

Pause.

Ju.

JULIE *steps out from behind the curtain.*

JULIE. Where is she?

BERNIE. Toilet.

JULIE. Stop talking to us then.

BERNIE. I just said. Don't bother! She's in a right mood.

The strap on that bag broke, you'll have to take it back, hope you've got the receipt.

JULIE. You know I haven't, it's off the market.

BERNIE. Well the strap broke.

ELLA *stands up from behind the sofa.*

ELLA. Mum. Stop talking to us.

BERNIE. I'm telling you, she's not in the mood.

JULIE. What are we doing then?

ELLA. Go out!

BERNIE *exits and closes the door.*

JULIE *and* ELLA *laugh.*

JULIE. So. We hiding or what?

ELLA. Might as well.

They hide again.

BERNIE *takes off her coat in the hall and adjusts her hair in the mirror.*

The sound of a toilet flushing.

BERNIE *opens the sitting-room door again.*

JULIE *jumps up.*

JULIE. Surprise!

BERNIE. She's just flushed.

ELLA *stands.*

BERNIE *goes out and closes the door again.*

JULIE. For fuck's sake.

They hide again.

MARY *comes out of the toilet, she undoes her coat but doesn't take it off.*

MARY. It smells funny in there.

BERNIE. Does it?

MARY *goes into the sitting room.*

JULIE *and* ELLA *jump out.*

JULIE/ELLA. Surprise!

BERNIE *enters behind her, rolling her eyes, her face a mixture of 'don't bother' and 'I told you'.*

MARY. What surprise, your coat's over the banister.

BERNIE. Are you going to have a sit-down before you unpack your bag?

Look, Ella's here to see you!

ELLA. Surprise!

BERNIE. That's nice, isn't it?

ELLA. Welcome home, Nana!

MARY. Yeah, well.

ELLA *kisses her,* MARY *lets her.*

BERNIE. You're not in the mood, are you, Mum? / Didn't I say she's in a mood.

MARY. I told you, I'm car sick.

JULIE. I took the afternoon off work you know! / I can't take pay for that

MARY. I'm not deaf, I can hear you.

JULIE. I know, I'm telling you, aren't I?

MARY. What you shouting for?

JULIE. Who's shouting? You'd know if I were shouting.

No one speaks for a moment. MARY *looks around the room.*

MARY. What's gone on in here?

BERNIE. Nothing.

We've got you your favourites in, for your tea and your snacks. Julie tidied round for you.

MARY *doesn't say anything.*

Gave it a hoover.

ELLA. Shall I make you a cup of tea, Nana?

BERNIE. She wants something to eat I expect. Shall Ella put a slice of toast in for you?

MARY. In a minute.

BERNIE. That's it, no rush is there.

Just taking it all in, aren't you? Adapting to being home.

JULIE *rolls her eyes and leaves the room.*

She goes into the kitchen.

MARY. She been staying here?

BERNIE. No.

MARY. She has.

BERNIE. Only for the odd night.

MARY. What's wrong with *her* house?

BERNIE. I don't know. She'll have to tell you that herself, won't she?

ELLA. Why don't you sit down, Nana?

BERNIE. Yeah.

MARY *leaves the room.*

MARY *goes upstairs into her bedroom, looks round the room and inside the wardrobe.*

BERNIE *and* ELLA *look at each other.*

She doesn't miss a trick, does she? God's sake. She's like bloody Poirot.

ELLA. What was it like? Did you have to wait ages?

BERNIE. Only half an hour or so.

ELLA. She looks old, doesn't she?

JULIE *comes in the room.*

JULIE. She's gone upstairs.

BERNIE. You better of put it all back the same.

Where you going to stay tonight?

JULIE. Here.

BERNIE makes a face 'really?'

Just till I get sorted.

BERNIE. You won't last five minutes.

JULIE. Jacko said I could stay at the pub if I'm desperate.

BERNIE. Jesus Christ, you'd have to be.

You can't stay at ours I've got no carpet upstairs till end of the month and Sanj is using the back room for bubble wrap.

ELLA. She's coming down.

No one says anything.

MARY comes back in.

JULIE. Alright, Mum?

MARY. No I'm not 'Alright, Mum' what's been going on in my house?

JULIE. Nothing, what do you mean?

MARY. Well, you've been living here for a start, he kick you out, did he?

JULIE. No.

ELLA leaves the room.

ELLA goes into the kitchen and makes a cup of tea.

MARY. Who's been messing about in my bedroom?

JULIE. No one.

MARY. Well, someone has, everything's been moved around and put back wrong.

JULIE. No it hasn't, like what?

MARY. All my pictures! All my bits and pieces. All my dresses and skirts have got mixed up in the cupboard, what's been going on?

BERNIE. You must of remembered it wrong.

MARY. Don't be making out it's me, I'm not going mad /

BERNIE. I never said you were / going mad

MARY. My cushions on the bed are upside down /

JULIE. I changed your bedding, I made it all nice for you!

MARY. Well, it's not nice is it? /

JULIE. Wish / I hadn't bothered!

MARY. Being lied to by your own daughters and taken advantage of.

JULIE. You what?

MARY. It's a miracle I haven't dropped dead of heart attack the stress I'm under, I've been in there over three months you know /

BERNIE. Come on / sit down

MARY. Moved around, treated like a criminal.

    BERNIE *and* JULIE *exchange glances*.

    You wouldn't last one night, you. You'd be screaming and shouting all sorts.

    I get out and now what? I'm being treated like an idiot in my own home /

JULIE. I've took the afternoon off work for this.

BERNIE. Come on, / sit down.

MARY. I've been dreaming of my own bed, I've had no privacy.

    BERNIE *steers* MARY *to sit down*.

    What you been sleeping in my bed for?

BERNIE (*to* JULIE). Just tell her.

    (*To* MARY.) You should work for MI5, you.

JULIE. I left him.

MARY. What for?

JULIE. Sick of it, weren't I.

MARY. Sick of what? Oh don't bother telling me I don't want
to know.

JULIE. Making me feel like shit all the time.

MARY *makes a 'so what?' face.*

MARY. Don't be thinking you can move in here.

JULIE. It's only till I get myself sorted.

MARY. Well, you can get yourself sorted somewhere else
because you're not doing it here.

JULIE. Right.

Thanks for your support.

MARY. You've had nothing *but* support, all your life. No one
forced you to drink you know, no one lifted the bottle to
your lips.

JULIE. Oh my god! Two minutes she's been home!

MARY. No one's supported you? / Who paid your car insurance
when you nearly lost your job because of it?

JULIE. I never said no one's supported me, I said thanks for
your support.

MARY. Moving all my precious things around.

You drinking again?

JULIE. No.

MARY. That why he kicked you out, was it?

ELLA *comes in with a mug of tea for* MARY.

BERNIE. Ella's come all the way across from Leeds, so are you
going to behave or what?

MARY *takes the tea*.

MARY. Thank you, love.

ELLA. Is it nice to be home, Nana?

MARY. Oh yeh.

BERNIE. She's in her third year now, aren't you?

ELLA. Yeah. Gone fast.

BERNIE. You're enjoying yourself, aren't you?

ELLA. Yeah it's good.

MARY. Not working too hard I hope.

ELLA. No.

MARY. That's good.

BERNIE. Hey, she can come to the graduation, can't she?
    You'd like that, wouldn't you, Mum? Day out in Leeds.

MARY. When's that then?

BERNIE. Summer, is it?

ELLA. I don't know how many tickets you're allowed, but
    yeah.

BERNIE. We only need three don't be daft, you'd like that,
    wouldn't you, Mum?

MARY. If I'm still here.

BERNIE. Where else you going to be?

MARY. Might be dead.

BERNIE. Don't be stupid.

    What you saying that for?

    It's something to look forward to, eh?

MARY. I was looking forward to getting in my bed tonight.

JULIE. Who's stopping you?

MARY. You. Sleeping in my room.

JULIE. For Christ's sake, you'd think I'd pissed in it.

MARY. Wouldn't put it past you.

BERNIE. I thought it were a bath you were looking forward to anyway.

No one will get in the bath with you, how about that?

No one says anything for a while.

MARY *drinks her tea.*

That's right, drink your tea.

BERNIE *and* JULIE *exchange glances.*

Is it nice?

MARY. Yeh.

BERNIE. Good.

Pause.

MARY (*to* JULIE, *sarcastic*). Thanks for coming to visit me.

JULIE. I was working, you know I was. I came when you were at Wakefield.

MARY. That were nearly six weeks ago, you've only got one mother, you know.

JULIE *and* BERNIE *look at each other, eye roll, small laugh.*

What you laughing for?

JULIE. I'm not.

MARY. What time's the shop shut?

BERNIE. The garage? It's twenty-four-hour you know it is.

MARY. I don't know anything, do I, it's all changed!

BERNIE. What has?

MARY. Launderette's all boarded up!

JULIE. You've got a washer-drier through there!

MARY. I know I have, I'm not senile.

BERNIE. What do you want a shop for anyway?

MARY. I need to get bits in, don't I?

BERNIE. We've done all that, finish your tea and I'll show you.

MARY. I'm meant to be having gammon. I had to fill out a canteen sheet – I told them I wouldn't be there but he said I had to fill it out anyway.

BERNIE. You're having salmon fillet with a sauce.

MARY *gives a look.*

That alright? You like salmon, don't you?

MARY. I expect you've drunk all my Baileys, have you?

JULIE. No.

Pause.

ELLA. There's a bottle of wine in the fridge.

BERNIE. Oh yeah, from the girls at work.

MARY. Whose work?

BERNIE. Mine.

ELLA. So you can have a little glass of white with your salmon, hey Nana?

MARY *doesn't say anything.*

BERNIE. That'll be nice, won't it.

MARY *doesn't say anything.*

Bloody hell, it's like trying to kick a horse up a hill.

MARY. I expect everyone knows, do they?

BERNIE. It was in all the papers of course they know.

MARY. Plenty to say about your dad I expect.

BERNIE. Yeah. Well.

MARY. Did you wash that muck off his gravestone?

No one answers.

Still on there, is it?

JULIE. We don't go up there.

MARY. Why not, he's still your dad.

BERNIE. You can't hardly read what it says.

It's really faint.

No one says anything.

MARY. It's all overgrown I expect, is it?

BERNIE. I don't know, we don't go up, she just said.

MARY. Well, I'm going up there tomorrow first thing.

BERNIE. Are ya?

MARY. Yes. And I'll take the stiff brush for the decking and I'll get that muck off if it kills me. I'll put some flowers on. I'll have it looking brand new.

BERNIE. Right.

MARY. And if anyone tries to stop me.

Pause.

ELLA. Are there still roadworks?

BERNIE. Oh yeah, you have to use the top gate to get in the cemetery now you can't get the 686 to right outside.

MARY. Bet it looks a right state.

BERNIE. Why don't you leave it for a few days, wait till you're settled back in and then go up?

MARY. I'm not having people thinking I'm ashamed.

Pause.

JULIE. Aren't ya? /

MARY. You what? /

BERNIE. God's sake, / Julie, don't start.

JULIE. Ashamed.

MARY. About what?

JULIE. Bloody hell, about what happened.

MARY. No!

BERNIE. Leave it! She's only just home.

JULIE. What, are we not allowed to mention it?

MARY. What have I got to feel ashamed about? I'm not the one made up a pack of lies, am I?

BERNIE. Let's get you settled, do you want Ella to fetch your slippers and dressing gown?

MARY. I'm not the one ruined a man's reputation, a man's good standing in the community he's lived in all his life. / Am I?

JULIE. He ran a minicab firm, he's not Gandhi.

MARY *gets up*.

MARY. Right that's it, go home, I've had enough.

BERNIE. Don't be daft we're not leaving you on your own.

MARY. Not you, her.

JULIE. And you wonder why I stopped coming to visit you? You've never changed.

MARY. I'm not having this.

JULIE. I thought you're s'posed to think things through when you're inside, come to terms with what you did wrong.

Not you, you still think the same as when you went in.

MARY. That's right and I'm not going to think anything different neither.

I got guilty for doing nothing. I got six months for saying nothing. There was nothing *to* say!

JULIE. It's a waste of time talking to you.

MARY. Is this how you speak to *your* mother, Ella, no I don't think so.

BERNIE. / Don't drag her into it

JULIE. What's she got to do with it?

MARY. I tell you what I *am* ashamed of – you.

Coming in stinking of drink with your knickers halfway up your back, shouting the place down, / banging on the door at four in the morning

JULIE. You what? When?

MARY. You know when! Falling on every man that so much as looked at you, no wonder Paul's kicked you out, / you're a liability

JULIE. He hasn't kicked me out, I walked out!

MARY. Staggered more like /

JULIE. You talking about when I was fifteen / and got drove home by the police?

MARY. You haven't changed, never mind you telling me I haven't changed /

JULIE. I'm forty-three now you know /

MARY. Everyone has a choice in life, don't they, make peace or make trouble. Well, we all know what you chose, don't we?

JULIE. Make peace? Oh you'd know about that, wouldn't ya?

MARY. You never stuck up for me in court.

It were you keeping your mouth shut made me look guilty, might as well of been you that locked the door of my cell every night!

Never coming to visit, I could of died in there and then what?

You'd of been happy then I expect.

Pause.

Yes. Born a waste of space and stayed a waste of space /

JULIE. Oh very nice!

ELLA. Do you want me to take your bag upstairs, Nana, and hang your things up?

MARY. The strap's broke – (*To* JULIE.) it's a load of rubbish.

BERNIE. I told her.

JULIE *shrugs*.

She can't take it back she hasn't got the receipt.

MARY. What did you have to sleep in my bed for?

BERNIE. Bloody hell is she still on this? Change the record.

MARY. That's a memory foam y'know, it remembers the shape of your body, they cost over four hundred pound. It's going to be in the shape of your body now, I'll be awake all night.

JULIE *and* BERNIE *laugh*.

All I wanted is a good night's sleep and you've taken that off me as well.

BERNIE. For god's sake, / this is priceless.

MARY. I'm still grieving your dad y'know, a professional Samaritan told me that. She said, 'You're not over the grieving process yet, Mary.'

BERNIE. What you doing ringing the Samaritans for?

MARY. You don't have to ring them, they come in, they listen to you.

BERNIE. That's good, isn't it?

MARY. Oh it's bloody brilliant, it's a real luxury!

You think I've been on a cruise.

BERNIE. No I don't.

Do you want me to put that salmon in for you? It's got
a watercress sauce, it looks nice.

MARY. I've got no appetite. I couldn't eat it.

BERNIE. You've got to eat something.

MARY. I should starve myself to death, do everyone a favour.

JULIE. She's saying stuff for attention now.

BERNIE. What you saying things like that for in front of Ella?

MARY (*to* ELLA). Don't ever get old, it's a living hell /

BERNIE. Oh don't listen to her.

MARY *cries, hides her face with her hands, no one
comforts her.*

MARY. When you've been through what I've been through, and
then you're just left. To get on with it on your own.

BERNIE. You're not on your own, are ya? What you saying
you're on your own for?

We're all stood here in front of your face! Julie's going to
stay with you. I'll be up in the morning, take you over to see
probation, have you text her?

MARY. How would I, you've got my phone in your bag.

BERNIE *hands her a tissue.*

BERNIE. Come on.

MARY *blows her nose.*

You can do whatever you like now, you can start again,
can't ya?

Hey?

You could get a little job. You could do a night class, be
a student like our Ella?

MARY. What would I wanna do a night class for?

BERNIE. To learn things you don't know! They do all sorts now.

They do Mandarin.

JULIE. They do over-sixties Zumba down the centre.

BERNIE. Why don't you get highlights done? It's half-price on a Thursday.

JULIE. You could get a dog!

MARY *pulls herself together.*

MARY. Oh what's the point?

No one's going to speak to me, are they?

BERNIE. Course they will.

MARY. Not after that bitch spread her lies around.

She's robbed my life off me! *She* should of got jail!

I won't be able to walk down the street now without people thinking those lies she said are true.

Beat.

JULIE. She's moved back you know.

BERNIE. What are you telling her that for?

JULIE. Because she has.

MARY. Moved back where?

JULIE. Here.

MARY. Tina's moved back here? When?

JULIE. About two month ago.

She's changed her name. They call her Briana now.

MARY. Briana? What kind of name's that?

JULIE. She changed it by deed poll. She had to go to City Hall.

Beat.

MARY. Well, you seem to know a lot about it.

JULIE. I've seen her around a couple of times. Yeh.

Beat.

MARY (*to* BERNIE). You've seen her as well I suppose.

BERNIE. I've seen her. Not to talk to.

I thought she'd want to stay as far away from here as she could to be honest.

So I was surprised.

To see her.

Pause.

MARY. Well.

MARY *turns her full attention to* ELLA.

You need to get back across to Leeds soon I expect, have you got uni tomorrow?

ELLA. I've got a reading week so I'm staying at home, I can get more work done here, there's less distractions.

BERNIE. She's sharing a flat with three boys, one of them's a drag queen, tell her.

BERNIE *leaves the room.*

BERNIE *goes into the kitchen and starts to prepare food.*

ELLA. He does an act where he's dressed as the girl who sang '99 Red Balloons', do you remember that song?

MARY. Oh yeah.

ELLA. Well, he does her.

MARY. Does he?

JULIE. Why?

ELLA. I don't know. He just really likes the song I think.

JULIE. Oh.

ELLA. He does it with ninety-nine real balloons so whenever he has a booking the front room's full of red balloons and every time you open the door they come out into the hall and through to the kitchen. They get under your feet. It drives you mad after a while.

JULIE. Why doesn't he wait till he gets to the venue to blow them up?

ELLA. I don't know, he should.

He uses same balloons over and over I think.

JULIE. What's his name?

ELLA. Ryan.

Silence.

Are you going to be okay, Nana?

MARY. Oh yeh.

ELLA. Do you want me to get your slippers for you?

MARY. Yes please, love, they're in the bottom of my cupboard, at least they *were*.

ELLA goes out.

ELLA goes upstairs into MARY's bedroom and gets the slippers.

JULIE. I'll put my stuff upstairs, shall I?

MARY turns her head away and doesn't answer.

It's bloody sweltering in here, have you got heating on?

MARY. I don't know, do I? Nothing to do with me. I'm a stranger in me own home.

JULIE takes her jumper off.

She's wearing a vest top underneath. Her arms and upper body are covered in dark purple and black bruises, deep marks from fingers pressed into her upper arms, stamp marks on her back.

MARY *doesn't react.*

JULIE *folds her jumper up neatly and puts it down.*

JULIE. Do you want me to get the TV guide for you?

MARY. What for, what am I gonna watch?

The door opens and BERNIE *comes back in.*

She looks at JULIE *and winces.*

BERNIE. Christ's sake, Julie, put your top back on before Ella sees you, look at the state of ya.

JULIE. It's sweltering, have you got heating on?

BERNIE. No! What you drawing attention to yourself for?

JULIE. I'm sweating like a pig.

BERNIE. A pig that's been beaten with a bloody iron bar! Cover yourself up.

JULIE puts her jumper back on.

Do you want peas or carrots with your salmon, Mum?

MARY. I don't want either, I told you, I've no appetite for it.

BERNIE *(to* JULIE*)*. Put telly on for her or something.

BERNIE *tuts and goes out.*

BERNIE *goes into the kitchen.*

MARY. If I find out Tina's stepped foot in this house while I've been locked up in that cell I swear to god. I will never call you my daughter again.

JULIE *holds her own. Says nothing.*

ELLA *comes in with Mary's slippers and drops them at her feet.*

ELLA. Shall I hang your coat up for ya, Nana?

MARY *stands and lets* ELLA *take off her coat.*

ELLA *takes* MARY*'s coat and bag into the hall.*

MARY. Did you hear what I said?

JULIE. Yeah.

MARY. So? Have you got something to say, because if you have say it.

JULIE. She's not called Tina any more. I told you, she's called Briana.

MARY *makes a face.*

MARY *puts on her slippers.*

You should see her.

MARY. I don't want to see her. /

JULIE. / She's changed.

MARY. And neither do you if you know what's good for you.

JULIE. It's like she's on fire and the flames won't be put out.

It's like she's a firework thrown on a fire.

MARY. What you trying to do?

JULIE. I'm not tryna do anything, I'm just telling you what she's like.

MARY. Are you trying to upset me?

JULIE. No.

MARY *turns her face away.*

Pause.

JULIE *gets the remote control and switches on the TV.*

MARY *gets up suddenly and leaves the room.*

Fade to black.

All of a sudden –

The front door bursts open and a shaft of light illuminates the house.

Silence.

2.

Mary's bedroom. Night.

MARY *is in a night dress sitting on the edge of her bed with a phone to her ear.*

MARY. Hello.

–

I don't know.

–

I probably shouldn't be ringing, I'm not suicidal or anything like that, I just.

–

Okay. Well.

–

Hello, Gillian.

–

Mary. That's my real name am I s'posed to give my real name or not I don't know how this works.

–

I don't know really, I.

–

I've been away and I just.

Long pause.

Are you still there?

Oh.

I probably shouldn't be ringing really I was just.

Is Sheila there? Do you know Sheila? I don't know her second name, she said she lived in Bradford. She's got curly blonde hair. Or it might have been Shirley, I think she had glasses.

–

Oh right.

–

Oh I didn't know that, right.

So you're not in Bradford then, I was gonna say, you don't sound like you're from round here.

–

It's only I lost my husband, it were three year ago in July but I'm still grieving y'know. It were three year ago in July, but.

And he was a miserable so-and-so as well, so I don't know why I'm even.

I'm better off!

So I don't know what I'm ringing for really. I was just wanting to say thank you to Shirley, y'know, for being nice.

She was really nice.

Pause. Then –

MARY *hangs up the phone abruptly.*

She sits still on the bed for a moment.

MARY *gets into bed and lies down.*

She takes a while to get comfortable before she switches off the light.

In the dark MARY *changes position in the bed.*

A moment passes.

MARY *switches the light back on.*

Pause.

What?

What do you want?

Pause.

MARY *switches off the light.*

3.

The middle of the night.

MARY *is asleep in her bed upstairs.*

The front door is open and in the hall is BRIANA. *She wears a poncho and long boots with a high heel.*

JULIE *is in the hall too, in a onesie.*

JULIE *speaks in hushed tones.*

BRIANA. Did you tell her I want to see her?

JULIE. Not yet.

BRIANA. What did she say?

JULIE. Nothing, I didn't tell her.

BRIANA. Did she ask if you'd seen me?

JULIE. No.

BRIANA. Did you tell her though?

JULIE. I don't think so, no.

BRIANA. Did you or not?

JULIE. No.

BRIANA. What and she didn't ask?

JULIE. No.

BRIANA. Really?

JULIE. Hang on, Bernie might of said something about it. That she'd seen you.

BRIANA. Did she?

JULIE. She said you'd changed your name.

BRIANA. Did she?

JULIE. Yeah that's what it was.

BRIANA. What did Mary say?

JULIE. Nothing. She went to bed early.

   Pause.

   She was in an upset mood.

BRIANA. Oh.

JULIE. You alright?

BRIANA. Have you got my laptop charger?

JULIE. Yeah. Shall I get it?

BRIANA. I might have a quick lie-down. A power nap.

JULIE. Here?

BRIANA. Yeah I might.

JULIE. Right.

BRIANA. What?

JULIE. You might wake her up. It might be a shock for her.

BRIANA. How can you wake someone up having a nap?

JULIE. She might wake up, come downstairs and see ya.

   I should tell her first. You could come round when she's got used to it.

BRIANA. I've got my application to write, it's the deadline tomorrow.

JULIE. She said she didn't want you to come to the house.

BRIANA. I thought she said nothing about me.

JULIE. I remember now. She did.

BRIANA. You're doing my head in, Julie. I don't know what's right and what's not.

   Pause.

JULIE. Shall I get your laptop charger?

BRIANA. Yeah.

JULIE *goes into the kitchen and unplugs a charger from the wall.*

BRIANA *goes into the front room.*

BRIANA *takes a pen out of her bag and writes 'Briana' on the wall beside the fireplace.*

JULIE *comes back into the front room.*

BRIANA *is setting up her laptop, she takes the charger from* JULIE *and plugs it in.*

JULIE. Have you got email back from Pierce Brosnan?

BRIANA. No. Nothing.

Nothing from Neil Morrissey, nothing from Kriss Akabusi.

JULIE. Tight fuckers.

BRIANA. Nothing from Kerry Katona, although I wasn't expecting anything from her / I think she's bankrupt.

JULIE. I was gonna say.

BRIANA. It's not a problem, I've got a plan B.

Well, it's my plan bloody L–M–N–O–P more like.

I'm filling out applications for all sorts.

I tell you what, when I'm rich I'm gonna give all my money away to social entrepreneurs.

JULIE. What about nurses?

BRIANA *doesn't answer. She's looking at the laptop screen.*

Paul keeps ringing me but I'm not answering my phone.

BRIANA. Good. Change your number.

He'll move on to some other pathetic weakling soon, forget him.

JULIE. I am trying to forget him but I keep thinking about him.

BRIANA. Have you had a drink?

JULIE. No.

BRIANA. See? You're stronger than you think.

JULIE. You can smell my breath.

BRIANA. I believe you.

>If you say you haven't had a drink then you haven't had a drink.

>Why would you say you hadn't had a drink if you'd had a drink? What have you got to gain?

>I don't care. Obviously I want you to be the best version of yourself you can be, but I'm not interested in making you feel bad.

>So that's good. That's nearly a fortnight, isn't it?

JULIE. Is it? / Something like that.

BRIANA. Well, nine days, ten days.

>Do you feel proud of yourself?

JULIE. I feel alright.

BRIANA. Give yourself a pat on the back for that, yeah?

JULIE. Yeah I s'pose.

BRIANA. Go on.

>JULIE *pats herself on the back.*

JULIE. It was easier when you were here. Took my mind off it.

BRIANA. I'm still here, aren't I?

JULIE. Yeh. But I mean staying here with me.

BRIANA. You don't fancy putting a boiled egg on for me, do you? Couple of soldiers?

JULIE. What if Mum wakes up?

BRIANA. I'll hide behind the settee. I'd probably fall asleep, I'm that tired!

>BRIANA *laughs.*

JULIE *doesn't say anything.*

Julie.

JULIE. What?

BRIANA. Show me your straight back.

JULIE. I'm fine!

BRIANA. I am not a victim. Say it.

JULIE. I'm just worried about upsetting her when she's only just home.

BRIANA. Say it.

JULIE. I am not a victim.

BRIANA. I may have been challenged, hurt, betrayed, beaten and discouraged but I am not defeated.

JULIE. I may have been challenged, hurt betrayed, whatever, I'm alright!

BRIANA. Beaten and discouraged.

JULIE. Beaten and discouraged.

BRIANA. But I am not defeated.

JULIE. Yeah I know! I am not defeated.

BRIANNA. I have been delayed but not denied.

JULIE. We should keep our voices down /

BRIANA. A positive present changes a negative past.

JULIE. The walls are like doilies.

BRIANA. Life changes every single second and so can I.

Julie, straight back.

JULIE *stands up straighter.*

The more I live, the more I learn, the more I realise how little I know.

Feeling incomplete is normal and healthy.

JULIE. It's the middle of the night, Bri, keep your voice down.

BRIANA *stops*.

BRIANA *changes her tone*.

BRIANA. I've kept my voice down for thirty-seven years. Ever since I spoke up and no one listened.

JULIE. I know.

BRIANA. I'm not doing that any more, Julie, I told you.

JULIE. Alright, I know.

BRIANA. You were there when I waited after school and told Miss Henshall, what did she say to me?

JULIE. I know.

BRIANA. She said, don't rock the boat, Tina, your dad won't like you saying those things, they'll send you back to Inglewood House, don't make trouble.

JULIE. I know.

BRIANA. Sometimes I think you don't know, it's like you don't remember.

I'm doing this for you an' all, you know.

JULIE. I know, thanks.

BRIANA. So did you tell Mary I'm Briana now.

JULIE. Yeh.

BRIANA. Did you tell her it means strong, virtuous and honourable.

JULIE. No.

BRIANA. Tell her.

JULIE. Is that what it means?

BRIANA. Yeah. Tell her please.

JULIE. Okay.

What does Julie mean?

BRIANA. And say I want to see her.

JULIE. Alright.

Probably means something stupid, does it?

BRIANA. Because I'm not that little girl any more, I won't apologise for speaking the truth.

I don't wish ill on Mary, I know why she did what she did. But I had to put it right.

JULIE. I'll tell her when she wakes up.

BRIANA. Yeh.

JULIE. When she's had a night's rest.

BRIANA. Because he may have thrown a lead blanket over the lot of us when he was alive, but he's dead now.

We don't have to lie under it for ever, do we?

JULIE. I'll tell her tomorrow.

BRIANA. Yeh.

I don't know what Julie means, I'll look it up when I've done this.

JULIE. Okay there's no rush.

BRIANA *goes back to her laptop screen.*

Bernie still hasn't got a clue about Ella dropping out of uni you know.

BRIANA *is concentrating on the screen.*

After a moment.

BRIANA. I need the loo.

JULIE. Use downstairs and don't flush.

BRIANA. Okay.

BRIANA *gets up and goes into the hall.*

BRIANA *goes straight upstairs.*

She opens the door to Mary's room very quietly and stands at the bottom of her bed watching her sleep.

Fade to black.

4.

Morning.

The bedroom upstairs is empty and the bed is neatly made.

In the front room JULIE *is sitting on the sofa in a onesie eating a bowl of cereal and looking at her phone.*

The TV is on.

BERNIE *comes through the front door with her coat on and her car keys in her hand.*

BERNIE *comes into the front room.*

BERNIE. Where is she?

JULIE. I dunno, she's not come down.

BERNIE. Did you take her a tea up?

JULIE. No.

BERNIE. You've sorted yourself out I see.

God's sake.

BERNIE *goes out into the hall.*

BERNIE *calls up the stairs.*

Mum!

Do you want a tea bringing up or are you coming down?

Silence.

JULIE *is looking at her phone.*

BERNIE *comes back into the front room.*

It's like time's stood still here.

BERNIE *opens the curtains and fixes the tie backs.*

What time you at work?

JULIE. One.

BERNIE. Who's in the office?

JULIE. No one.

BERNIE. Since when?

JULIE. They're fine. It's quiet in the mornings. I've cut the
drivers by half, the phones are dead, I've told ya.

BERNIE. Don't talk to me, I've had no sleep. Has she been in
the shower?

JULIE. I dunno.

BERNIE. Did you hear the hot water go on?

JULIE. No.

BERNIE. Bloody hell, we're going to be late for her
appointment if we don't get a move on, they can put you
straight back inside y'know, if you're late.

JULIE. Don't be stupid.

BERNIE. They can! What *you* doing anyway, I thought you
were going to sort somewhere to stay.

JULIE. I know.

BERNIE. You can't stay here, she'll drive you into the ground,
you know she will.

JULIE. Paul keeps messaging me.

BERNIE. Saying what?

JULIE. Being nice. Asking me what I want for my birthday.

BERNIE. Tell him a suicide note.

JULIE. He's gonna do anger management.

BERNIE. He put his name down for that before remember, and when he got there he couldn't find a parking space and ended up lamping some disabled bloke outside Morrisons.

BERNIE *laughs*, JULIE *doesn't*.

JULIE. He wasn't disabled, he was using his wife's blue badge.

BERNIE. Why you don't just kick him out I don't know.

ELLA *comes in the front door and into the front room*.

ELLA. What's happening?

BERNIE. Nana's not even down yet.

BERNIE *goes out, she goes upstairs*.

BERNIE *goes into* MARY*'s bedroom, sees the empty bed, before returning downstairs*.

JULIE. How long you gonna say your reading week goes on for? Six months?

ELLA. No.

I'm gonna tell her at the weekend.

JULIE. She'll clock you're not reading an' all.

ELLA. Who says I'm not reading, I read all the time.

JULIE. You gonna tell me what went on?

ELLA. No.

JULIE. What you saying No like that for? Don't you trust me?

ELLA. I don't want to talk about it.

JULIE *makes a 'fair enough' face*.

JULIE. Did you see photo Becky put up on Instagram?

ELLA. Of her dog in a wig, yeah.

JULIE. I nearly choked.

ELLA. I know. Hilarious.

BERNIE *comes back in.*

BERNIE. She's not upstairs. Her bed's made.

JULIE. Is it?

BERNIE. Where is she?

JULIE. I would have heard her go out.

BERNIE. Well, you obviously wouldn't cos she's gone out and you heard nothing, so, maybe put the career as a private detective on hold for the moment.

Or at least till you can go a night without a drink.

JULIE. I didn't have a drink last night.

BERNIE. Yeah, right.

Well, you've lost me mother.

JULIE. She's free to go out, she's not on a tag.

BERNIE. What did you have to go and tell her Tina's back for, / I thought we said we were gonna say nothing?

JULIE. Briana.

BERNIE. Bloody Briana whatever, I thought we said?

JULIE. Yeah I forgot.

BERNIE. She doesn't need it, Julie. Don't blame me if she has a heart attack from stress, you'll be able to thank yourself for that.

Bloody forgot. We only said it yesterday.

JULIE. Someone's gonna tell her, it's better it comes from us.

BERNIE. Who's gonna tell her? Everyone else's got more sense. It's only you with screw loose.

'Oh alright Mary, how was it inside? By the way, y'know your step-daughter what got you sent down well I saw her in the pub, bold as brass.'

Think before you speak, will you?

ELLA. Where's she been staying?

BERNIE. Who, Tina? Don't ask.

JULIE. Briana.

BERNIE. Oh shut up.

JULIE. She changed it by deed poll, it's her *name*.

BERNIE. I don't care. I'm gonna call her Tina because I've known her as Tina since I were three-year-old, what you gonna do, report me?

Eh? Who to?

Bloody. Name police?

You can change your name all you like but you're still same person, aren't ya?

What time is it?

ELLA. Five past.

BERNIE. This is getting silly now.

ELLA. Maybe she's gone up the cemetery.

JULIE. Yeah, like she said she were gonna.

BERNIE. What's she gone up there by herself for?

JULIE. She's allowed to go up there if she wants. Chill out.

BERNIE. Someone has to look after her, she's an old lady!

JULIE. I know! That's why I'm stopping here with her, aren't I?

BERNIE. Don't make out that's you being good, it's only cos you've had a bust up with bloody Fred West, it's all about *you*. And what suits *you*.

No one can believe I'm the youngest y'know.

JULIE. You what?

BERNIE. Me dad would still be waiting to be buried if it were down to you to sort it.

JULIE (*to* ELLA). Can you hear this?

BERNIE. Leave her alone. Get some clothes on, you're like a big baby in that thing.

How you've been mother to three children I will never know – *useless* you are.

ELLA *moves to the window and looks out.*

JULIE. I did everything for my boys you bloody know I did /

BERNIE. Oh right, did ya?

JULIE. It's not my fault what happened with Michael.

BERNIE. We're going to miss this appointment and it won't be my fault either, I was here for eleven. And I'm taking holiday for this y'know /

JULIE. I could of taken her!

BERNIE. Could ya? You can't make her a cup of tea! She's went missing before you've even got dressed!

JULIE. You said you wanted to do it.

BERNIE. Lucky I did!

You're about as much use as a gonk on a blunt pencil.

Pause. She feels bad.

Have you heard from Michael?

JULIE. You know I haven't.

BERNIE. Alright, I'm only asking!

Pause.

So he hasn't text you then?

JULIE s*hakes her head.*

Oh well, I expect he'll be in touch when he wants something.

ELLA (*looking out the window*). She's here.

BERNIE. Thank god / for that.

JULIE. See. Bloody drama.

ELLA. There's someone with her.

BERNIE/JULIE. Who?

ELLA. A woman.

BERNIE. Who is it?

ELLA. I don't know her.

JULIE. What woman?

The front door open, MARY enters with LEIGH.

LEIGH is wearing an anorak over a dress with bare legs and high-heeled mules, her face is dirty, she looks like a baby bird that's fallen out of a nest.

She is holding a sleeping bag and a bundle of clothes spilling out of a split bin bag.

MARY. In you come that's right.

LEIGH wipes her feet.

Go in, you're alright.

LEIGH stands in the doorway of the front room, she stares blankly at JULIE and BERNIE. They look back at her but don't say anything.

ELLA. Alright.

LEIGH tips her head slightly but doesn't say anything.

MARY comes in behind LEIGH.

BERNIE. Where've you been, you've got your appointment at twelve.

MARY. I know.

(*To LEIGH.*) Sit down, love.

LEIGH *sits on the edge of the sofa.*

I know I've got my appointment at twelve that's why I'm
back here for eleven.

BERNIE. It's five past.

BERNIE *throws a look at* JULIE.

We didn't know where you were.

MARY (*to* LEIGH). Do you want me to cook you a breakfast
before I go?

LEIGH. Yes please, Mary, thank you.

LEIGH *flicks her eyes up at everyone and then back down
again. She's holding the bag close.*

MARY. Shall I put that lot in the wash?

LEIGH. Yes please. Thank you. If it's not too much bother.

MARY *takes the bag from her.*

It's a bit. It stinks.

MARY. That's alright, love, give it here.

LEIGH. Yeh. Thank you, Mary.

MARY *takes the bag into the kitchen.*

After a moment, BERNIE *leaves the room and follows*
MARY *into the kitchen.*

JULIE *follows soon after.*

LEIGH *and* ELLA *are left in the front room.*

In the kitchen, MARY *moves efficiently between fridge, stove
and washing machine.*

BERNIE. What's going on, who's that?

MARY. Leigh. / Mind out.

BERNIE. Who's Leigh?

MARY. Leigh. We worked in the library together.

BERNIE. What library, you never worked in a library.

MARY. In New Hall, I told you.

JULIE *enters the kitchen.*

JULIE. Who the bloody hell's she?

BERNIE. Leigh from library in New Hall.

JULIE. She looks like she's on crack what have you brought her in the house for?

MARY. You look like you're on crack, I can't get rid of you.

BERNIE. You've got probation at twelve /

MARY. I know! I'm only doing a egg sandwich.

JULIE. How / long's she staying for?

BERNIE. Never mind bed and breakfast, if you're late they'll send you straight back in.

MARY. She's had no sleep for three nights, she's wrung out like a cloth.

JULIE. So is she just going to eat that and get off?

MARY. She can stay as long as she likes.

JULIE. You don't even know her!

MARY. Yes I do.

BERNIE. What was she inside for?

JULIE. Where's she gonna sleep?

MARY *doesn't say anything. She is breaking eggs into a pan.*

JULIE *and* BERNIE *throw a look at each other.*

In the front room, LEIGH *is leaning forward rolling a cigarette.*

LEIGH. Are you the one, you go college?

ELLA. In Leeds yeah.

LEIGH. So you're dead clever, wait, did you dye your hair?

ELLA. Yeah, I had blonde streaks last year.

LEIGH. Uh?

ELLA. Yeah, it was blonde, before.

LEIGH. Yeh I know. I saw it on the pictures. She had it on her noticeboard.

In the kitchen BERNIE *and* JULIE *are watching* MARY *frying an egg.*

BERNIE. We need to get a move on, Mum. Traffic's all backed up cos of roadworks.

MARY *doesn't respond, she carries on frying the eggs.*

In the front room.

ELLA. So were you in...?

LEIGH. You're pretty, you know?

ELLA. Thanks.

LEIGH. Not just a pretty face.

You the brains in the family then, yeh?

ELLA. Not really.

LEIGH. Yes you are.

Pause.

I'm the arse.

ELLA. Oh yeh?

LEIGH *laughs*

LEIGH. Do you know what I mean?

BERNIE *leaves the kitchen and comes into the hall. She beckons to* JULIE *to follow her.*

JULIE *and* BERNIE *have a whispered, over-articulated conversation in the hall.*

BERNIE. What the hell's going on?

JULIE. I know!

BERNIE. Are you thinking what I'm thinking?

JULE. What?

BERNIE. Do you smell a bloody rat?

JULIE. I dunno, yeh.

BERNIE. She's getting taken for a ride! It's obvious.

(*Loud enough for* MARY*'s benefit.*) If we don't leave now we're going to be late. It's thirty-nine minutes on the satnav and that's before traffic and parking.

BERNIE *mouths 'Get her out'.*

She mimes for JULIE *to go into the front room and talk to* LEIGH.

JULIE *mimes 'no way'.*

BERNIE *goes to the doorway to the front room.*

LEIGH *finishes rolling the cigarette.*

LEIGH *looks up and sees* BERNIE.

You can't smoke in the house.

LEIGH *lights it.*

Did you hear what I said?

LEIGH. Yeh.

LEIGH *stands up.*

I'm going outside.

BERNIE. Right.

Silence as ELLA *and* BERNIE *watch* LEIGH *leave the room.*

LEIGH *stops at the door.*

LEIGH. Can you see I'm not wearing any knickers?

BERNIE *and* ELLA *look away.*

LEIGH *turns round and bends over.*

Can you see now?

BERNIE. Oh that's very nice.

LEIGH *laughs.*

LEIGH *moves out into the hall,* JULIE *is standing in the hall.*

JULIE *watches* LEIGH *as she goes out through the front door.*

Fade to black.

The very loud, abstracted sound of the washing machine on a spin cycle.

Then the door to the box room slowly opens by itself throwing light across the bed in there.

5.

Later that afternoon.

BERNIE *is in the front room in her coat.*

She is looking at the wall by the fireplace where BRIANA *has written 'Briana', she is trying to get it off by spitting on the end of her scarf and rubbing it, while speaking on the phone.*

BERNIE. I don't know, felt tip or something, it won't come off!

–

When?

–

Never mind a text! You better get looking and find her as soon as you finish work and tell her to her face that that's not an option, Julie.

–

Because she's not ready for it!

I'm rubbing the paper off here. We'll need the whole room redoing at this rate.

MARY *is standing in the hall at the bottom of the stairs.*

LEIGH *is standing on the staircase.*

MARY. I thought you were going to have a lie-down.

LEIGH. I can't sleep in there, Mary.

MARY. You've had no sleep for three days you should be out like a light.

LEIGH. I don't like that room, I can't sleep in that room.

MARY. Why not?

LEIGH. I don't know, I can't. / I wanna lie on the settee.

MARY. What's wrong with it?

LEIGH. I dunno, I can't explain. It's bad for my chest. Shall I go your room, not under the cover, on the cover, on the top.

I'll smooth it over after, I won't mess it.

MARY. What's wrong with the small room?

LEIGH. Mary! I've fucking told you, It's giving me anxiety. I can't get my breath in that room.

MARY. Have you opened the window?

LEIGH. My fucking throat's closing, / I'm not making it up you know.

MARY. Alright.

LEIGH. Why are you being so fucking awkward?

MARY. I know you're not making it up.

LEIGH. Fuck's sake.

MARY. Go in my room.

LEIGH. You know I'm not making it up, don't ya, Mary.

MARY. Take the duvet off the single.

LEIGH. Thank you, Mary, I don't want to be a bother, am I?

MARY. You're alright.

LEIGH. Sorry! Don't kick me out. / I said sorry, I'm sorry alright?

MARY. You can stay as long as you like, I told you, didn't I.

LEIGH. You know I proper appreciate this.

MARY. Yeh.

LEIGH. No, honest to god, Mary, you're the only person I can turn to, you know that, don't you?

MARY. I know, love, yeh, get some sleep.

LEIGH. I know what I were gonna say, did they write back about the crisps, did you get more different flavours?

MARY. Nothing happened. No one said.

LEIGH. That was a good letter we did.

I bet they get more flavours any day now. Smoky bacon or something.

I bet they sit round eating them. Saying, about the letter.

That's cos of me and you you know!

MARY. Go and lie down and I'll bring you a cup of tea in a bit.

LEIGH. Is my washing done?

MARY. It's not hung up yet.

LEIGH. I'll lie on your bed.

MARY. Okay, love.

LEIGH *walks back upstairs.*

LEIGH. I can't sleep in that room, there's a bad energy or something in that room I swear to god.

LEIGH *goes into* MARY*'s room and lies on the bed.*

MARY *comes into the front room.*

MARY. You're off now, are you?

BERNIE. I'm going in work.

> There's a leaving do for one of the TAs tonight and if I don't show my face for work I can hardly just turn up for the drinks, can I?

> MARY *makes a face*.

> What?

MARY. I thought you said you wanted to hand your notice in anyway.

BERNIE. How do you think I'm going to get Ella through uni on two days doing accounts for Dixie's, we're down to six drivers on a weekend y'know.

MARY. Julie's running it into the ground by the looks of it.

> She's not even been in.

BERNIE. Where do you think she is now? Anyway. It's not cos of Julie.

MARY. What's it cos of then?

> BERNIE *doesn't answer*.

> It were doing fine before.

> BERNIE *doesn't answer, shakes head, rolls eyes*.

> What's that face for?

BERNIE. Nothing. (*Indicating* LEIGH *upstairs*.) How long before she slings her hook?

MARY. What's it got to do with you, it's my house.

BERNIE. I'm only asking! She's got you running round after her like she's Meghan Markle.

> You should be concentrating on yourself.

MARY. You don't know you're born compared to what she's been through. They locked her in a garage for a week you know, she had all sorts done to her.

They took all her clothes off her, chucked her in the boot of a car, drove her down the M6 in the middle of the night and slung her into a skip like a bag of rubbish.

BERNIE. Oh yeah?

Is that what she got jail for, fly-tipping?

She could be telling you anything.

MARY. She has nightmares every night, she'd wake the whole landing up with screaming.

BERNIE. Anyone can scream, screaming proves nothing.

MARY. One thing I do know, she's got no one to care for her.

And I've got no one to care *for*, so. There we are.

BERNIE. What you on about, you've got a family of your own to care for!

MARY. Who? None of you listen to a word I say, why should I care for you?

BERNIE. Are you joking?

MARY. Julie never even bothered to come and see me, none of you spoke up for me in court, / I don't want to get into it –

BERNIE. How could we of spoke up for you? It's a court of law not the top of a bus, / what did you want us to do?

MARY. I don't want to get into it, I'm done and dusted. I know where I stand thank you, I'm on my own, as long as I know, / that's fine.

BERNIE. Give over saying you're on your own –

MARY. I'm used to it, I've been on my own for the last twelve and a half weeks! You try going inside for crimes against a child, no one talks to ya!

BERNIE. What about your best mate upstairs?

MARY. She was the only one that'd have anything to do with me, she stuck her neck out.

Not like you lot.

You couldn't wait for your dad to die so you could all turn on me.

BERNIE. What you saying that for?

MARY. Kicking me when I'm down. Not telling me things.

I know what's going on you know. / Talking behind my back.

BERNIE. What? What's going on? I must be doing whatever it is behind my own back, because I don't know what you're on about.

MARY. Leigh wrote me a card y'know, saying how she wished I was her mother. Well, you know what, I wish she was my daughter an' all.

Instead of you devious lot.

BERNIE. You're just being offensive now.

MARY. I do! She was a better daughter to me those six weeks in New Hall /

BERNIE. I beg your pardon? / That's rich that is –

MARY. You heard. You wanna grow up you do.

BERNIE. Do I? I've been the most mature adult in this house since I were six!

Beat.

So, what were she in for?

MARY. That's none of your business.

BERNIE. Yeah. Well, let's hope it's not.

MARY. What's that supposed to mean?

BERNIE. I don't want to be walking in here and finding you with your throat cut and your handbag gone.

MARY. Yeh and you'd be more worried about my handbag an' all.

Pause.

BERNIE. Of course we care about you, we're your family, aren't we?

Beat. BERNIE *looks at her watch.*

I've got to go, I'm gonna be late now.

Silence.

You know when we were kids and you used to let us watch telly in your bed in the morning sometimes, at the weekends, and then all of a sudden you just stopped and said we couldn't come in any more. Do you remember that, Mum?

MARY *doesn't say anything.*

Mum.

MARY. What?

BERNIE. Do you remember it?

MARY *stands.*

Where you going?

MARY. Am I not free to stand up in my own house now?

BERNIE. Course you are.

Pause.

MARY. My mouth's dry, I can't swallow.

MARY *goes into the kitchen.*

BERNIE *waits for a moment, then, she gets up and leaves the house.*

Fade to black.

An outline of JULIE *standing in the dark at the window in the front room on the phone to Paul.*

A whispered, drunken spiral of muffled conversation that gradually slides into silence.

JULIE. No, listen, listen, Paul, I'm trying to tell you something... I can't explain it... I do and I don't... Listen to me... How do I know it's not gonna go back to how it were?... No... I never said that, when did I say that... I can't come home, can I... you know why, I can't, Paul... because it won't work... I'm not coming over... because I'm not that's why...

Then quiet.

6.

Sudden loud scream.

The bedside light in Mary's room is switched on.

LEIGH *is sitting bolt upright in the bed, screaming, and* BRIANA *is sitting on the bed next to her.*

BRIANA *is watching her, not making any effort to calm her or stop her screaming.*

MARY *is in the spare room, she sits up in bed, then comes out of the room onto the landing.*

MARY. Leigh, stop it, it's a dream, you're in the house.

Downstairs, the light switches on in the front room, JULIE *sits up from sleeping on the sofa covered in a coat.*

MARY *appears in the doorway of her bedroom,* LEIGH *stops screaming.*

LEIGH. Who the fuck is she? Who is she? Get her out of my room!

BRIANA. Hello Mary.

MARY. How did you get in? / Get out my house, now.

BRIANA. Did Julie tell you I wanted to see you?

MARY *(calls)*. Julie!

BRIANA. Mary, I just want to talk to you.

JULIE *stands up from the sofa, she is disorientated. She comes to the foot of the stairs and calls up.*

JULIE. What?

MARY. Tina's got in the house, call Bernie!

MARY *comes down the stairs quickly, she is followed by* BRIANA *walking slowly.*

MARY *pushes past* JULIE *who falls slightly into the banister.*

BRIANA. I'm not Tina, Mary, I'm Briana. I come in peace /

MARY. Well, you can get out! This is my house and you're trespassing on private property.

(*To* JULIE.) She's broke in tell her, she needs to get here *now*.

JULIE. Wait, what?

BRIANA. I never broke in, I walked in, the front door was open.

MARY. You're a bloody liar, why would the front door be open in the middle of the night? Julie, call Bernie I said.

LEIGH *has come to the top of the stairs and watches.*

BRIANA. I just want to talk, there's nothing to be scared of, / I just want to talk, calmly.

MARY. I'm not scared of you, you're the one that should be scared of me /

BRIANA. Well, I'm not scared of anything any more, Mary, I'm Briana now. I told Julie to tell you.

JULIE (*to* BRIANA). I was looking for you, Paul said he'd seen you in The Three Bells.

BRIANA *moves into the front room, she takes off her poncho and sits on the sofa.*

MARY. Oi! Where are *you* going?

MARY *follows her in.*

Excuse me /

BRIANA. I'm not a threat to you, I only want to talk.

MARY. You're off your head on something.

BRIANA. I'm seven years clean in September, Mary, you heard my solicitor tell them in court.

MARY. You've got three seconds to get out my house.

BRIANA. I'm not going anywhere.

BRIANA *stares straight ahead.*

MARY *stands in the doorway for a moment.*

MARY. Right. (*Calls.*) Julie!

MARY *leaves the room.*

JULIE *is coming out of the downstairs toilet.*

What you doing hiding in there for? Have you called her?

JULIE. Who?

MARY. Jesus Christ, Julie, have you got any sense left in your head that hasn't been knocked out, Bernie!

JULIE. Right.

MARY *walks up the stairs and past* LEIGH *into her bedroom.*

LEIGH. Who is she?

MARY. You come in here with me.

LEIGH *follows her in.*

MARY *shuts the door and looks around the room for something to barricade the door.*

MARY *tries to move a bedside table.*

LEIGH. Who is she though?

MARY. No one. Help me with this.

LEIGH. I thought I was going have a heart attack. It was like a horror film in my head. I thought she were going to stab me with a screwdriver.

LEIGH watches MARY move the table against the door.

The framed photos on the surface all fall. LEIGH picks one up.

Downstairs BRIANA and JULIE are listening to the sound of the furniture being moved.

JULIE. I were gonna tell her you wanted to see her but she went to bed early, I was gonna tell her in the morning first thing.

She's moving something in front of the door now.

BRIANA. I'll stay here till she comes down, I'm in no rush.

JULIE. Did you write Briana on the wall over there?

BRIANA. I just want to be part of life.

JULIE. Cos Bernie saw it.

BRIANA. Who's that girl?

JULIE. I'm gonna ring Bernie. Me mum's locked herself in her room. She'll go mad about this.

BRIANA. What's she doing sleeping in Mary's room for?

JULIE. Was she?

JULIE goes to the foot of the stairs and calls up.

Mum! Have you locked yourself in the room?

There's no answer.

Fuck's sake.

Upstairs MARY stands listening at the door, she's shaken.

LEIGH *lies on the bed.*

MARY. I'm gonna stay up here till she's out and the door's locked behind her.

Cos I don't want to know, Tina! I don't want to hear it.

LEIGH. Do you want me to go downstairs and tell her, Mary?

MARY. She can't let it rest, can she? Ray wasn't dead two days when the solicitor's letter came through letterbox saying she's raked it all back up again.

LEIGH. I'll go down there if you like I'm not bothered.

MARY. I'd been a widow two days! She's still banging the same drum!

LEIGH. I got a bad vibe off her.

MARY. I'll get the police on her /

LEIGH. No you're not.

MARY. The police know all about her, oh yeh.

She's a devious little bitch.

Downstairs JULIE *comes into the front room on the phone.*

JULIE (*on phone*). She's gone and locked herself in her room with the girl from New Hall.

–

I don't know.

Briana's here.

–

I didn't.

–

Ends call.

(*To* BRIANA.) She's coming over.

BRIANA. I told you to tell Mary I'm Briana now.

JULIE. I told her last night!

BRIANA. Did you tell her I'm sorry she got a custodial sentence, because my lawyers were surprised at that, / they thought she'd get a suspended.

JULIE. I told her yeh.

BRIANA. My heart's going like the clappers.

JULIE. Do you want a drink?

BRIANA. You've had a few, haven't you?

JULIE. Only cos I was looking for you! Paul text me you were in The Three Bells, that's the only reason I went in there.

BRIANA. I'm gonna sit here till she comes down, / 'I am not a victim'.

JULIE. I only went in there cos of looking for you!

BRIANA. 'I may have been challenged, hurt, betrayed, beaten and discouraged but I am not defeated.'

JULIE. So, do you want a drink or not?

BRIANA sits with a straight back and her eyes closed.

A moment.

JULIE stands.

I might.

BRIANA opens her eyes.

BRIANA. I've waited this long to hear her say she believes me, I'm in no rush.

JULIE. Is that what you want because she's never gonna say that y'know.

BRIANA. She will. I've visualised it.

Beat.

JULIE. She's never gonna say it.

BRIANA. Don't you want that an' all, Julie?

JULIE. What?

BRIANA. What would it mean to you if she looked you in the eyes and said, Julie, I know what happened to you and I'm sorry I never did anything about it?

JULIE (*recoils*). No, I don't want that.

BRIANA. Well, you should want it.

JULIE. I don't! Don't tell me what I should or shouldn't, fuck off.

BRIANA. You deserve it.

JULIE. Fuck off, what do you know about me anyway?

BRIANA *looks at* JULIE *for a moment and then turns away.*

BRIANA. I know loads.

JULIE. Yeh? You fucking think you do.

You think you know it fucking all, don't ya? Fucking *'talking'* and, fucking...

BRIANA *gets up.*

(*Ugly.*) Yeah that's right fuck off, no one wants you back here.

No one's ever wanted you. When you gonna get the message?

BRIANA *moves a table away from under the window, clears some space.*

What you doing that for now?

BRIANA *moves to one end of the sofa.*

BRIANA. Get the other end.

JULIE. What?

BRIANA. Get the other end, pick it up.

JULIE. What for?

BRIANA. Lift it.

JULIE. Why?

BRIANA. Just do it. Help me.

JULIE *takes the other end of the sofa.*

They lift it and BRIANA *steers it into the centre of the room, manoeuvring it round into a new position under the window.*

Underneath the original sofa position is a large dark stain.

The sofa was here before, under the window, remember?

JULIE. So?

BRIANA. Mary moved it to cover that.

They look at the stain.

It's from when I first said what were going on and no one listened to me. My dad smacked my head off the mantelpiece for it, I bled on the carpet.

JULIE *acknowledges this with her face like no big deal.*

If this house could speak.

BRIANA *sits back down on the sofa in its new position.*

There's holes in the doors upstairs from if you woke him up after a night shift, there'll be my tooth he knocked out, in between the floorboards somewhere.

JULIE. You'll never find that.

BRIANA. Mary can lie in court, she can pervert course of public justice as much as she likes, makes no difference. It's all here.

This house is my witness.

JULIE. Should of took the house into court with ya, shouldn't ya.

BRIANA. Mary knows what happened here, and she knows she knows, and she knows I know she knows.

JULIE. What about a punch in the nose to go with it?

Pause.

Move it back, it looks awful.

BRIANA. I'm gonna get her to say she believes me.

JULIE. Good luck.

BRIANA. I will, I'm gonna get her to say it.

JULIE. I know! I heard ya the first time, I said good luck.

Silence.

BRIANA. Why you're taking it out on me for? I kept my promise, didn't I? I promised I'd never say about you and I didn't, did I? All through the trial. Even though it would of helped my case. I kept my promise.

JULIE shrugs. She moves to the door and out into the hall, she goes to the foot of the stairs.

JULIE (*calls up*). Mum!

Bernie's coming over!

Pause.

(*Muttering.*) Well, I don't know about you but.

JULIE goes into the kitchen and opens the wine from the fridge.

She pours a glass, drinks the whole glass, then pours another glass and takes a sip.

She puts the bottle back in the fridge.

Upstairs, LEIGH is in the bed looking at MARY's framed photographs.

MARY is standing by the door, listening.

LEIGH. I'm cold, Mary, put heating on, will ya?

Is that you?

MARY. Stop putting your fingers on the glass, you're getting marks all over.

LEIGH. What did you marry *him* for?

He looks old. He looks like he wants to get sucked off.

MARY (*stern. Gives her a look*). Leigh.

LEIGH. What? He does!

MARY *moves to the window and looks out.*

MARY. It's Julie, letting her come round here, she thinks I don't know.

LEIGH. She was gonna stab you in your face when you were asleep y'know, she thought I was you / I swear to god.

MARY. While I'm locked up for doing nothing!

LEIGH *rolls a cigarette from her tobacco on the bedside table.*

There's a light on at Sandra's. They're all twitching their curtains, having a good look, thinking all sorts. I don't care, they can think what they like.

LEIGH. I bet he had a little two-inch cock, did he?

MARY. They'll be nice to my face, but they're using the cab firms from Idle now I bet, wouldn't put it past them.

LEIGH. I bet it was one of them like a chip stick, I bet it was one of them you can't hardly feel if it's up you, was it? Dead thin.

MARY. What?

LEIGH. His cock.

MARY (*makes face*). Don't talk like that, Leigh.

It's not nice, you let yourself down.

Pause.

Remember your list.

LEIGH. No, Mary, I'm not doing the list any more, I don't want to open a tea shop in the countryside, I don't know why I even said that.

Downstairs, BRIANA *gets up from the sofa suddenly and runs upstairs.*

MARY *moves to the door.*

MARY. She's coming up.

BRIANA *pushes the door open, the dressing table starts to move,* LEIGH *tries to sit on it but she's not fast enough and* BRIANA *gets into the room.*

What the hell do you think you're doing?

BRIANA. Mary. / Listen to me.

LEIGH (*shouts*). Fuck off out of our room! /

MARY (*calls*). Julie!

BRIANA. I understand why you lied in your witness statement in 1993, okay, and I forgive you.

LEIGH *tries to push* BRIANA *out of the room,* BRIANA *pushes back.*

MARY. I'm not having this –

BRIANA. You were under pressure from my dad –

MARY *pushes past them and out of the room.*

Please, Mary, I know you were.

That's why you lied, it's okay, I just want you to say it to me –

MARY *comes down the stairs.*

MARY. Right, that's it now.

LEIGH *tries to pin* BRIANA *down on the bed to stop her following but she's strong and breaks free and follows* MARY *down.*

BRIANA. Because – Can you listen to me please, Mary – what happened – okay? – with no one listening to me, no one hearing me – or believing me.

I shrank, basically – into a very fragile and fearful place –

MARY (*calling*). / Where's Julie?

BRIANA. – and it's taken twenty years of self-care – of rebuilding /

MARY (*she looks round the door into the front room*). What's gone on here? / Who's moved my settee?

BRIANA. For me to know, right, that nothing that happened to me in the first sixteen years of my life was my fault.

Upstairs, LEIGH *smashes one of the pictures.*

MARY (*calls*). Julie!

JULIE *comes out of the kitchen into the hall.*

(*To* JULIE.) I blame you for this.

JULIE. Makes a change /

MARY. Look at the state of you, I knew you were drinking again. / Where's Bernie?

JULIE. I'm not!

BRIANA. Mary. Can me and you just have a talk – adult to adult, can we?

JULIE. I haven't had a drink for a fortnight, have I, Briana? I got a pat on the back for it.

LEIGH *comes to halfway down the stairs, she is holding something behind her back.*

BRIANA. That's all I want, I never wanted you to get sent down you know, I told Julie to tell you, didn't I?

MARY (*to* JULIE). What did I say to you? Bring her back under my roof and that's it.

JULIE. I know! I were looking for her to tell her not to come round here again, / I've been all over.

MARY. I mean it, Julie, you can go back to Paul I don't care.

BRIANA. Julie, tell her.

MARY. I'll call the police on the both of you, never mind 'tell her', she's got nothing to tell me.

BRIANA. Yes she has, haven't you, Julie?

JULIE. No. (*Small laugh.*) I don't know what you're on about.

BRIANA. You do.

MARY. You put words into people's mouths, make everyone a liar like you.

BRIANA. There's nothing to be scared of, Julie, we'll stand together.

JULIE. I'm not scared, I don't know what you're talking about, that's all.

BRIANA. I've found love in my heart for you, Mary –

MARY. / I don't want your love thank you very much.

BRIANA. – that'll probably come as a surprise to you. I've had to dig deep and find the love because I had that much bitterness and rage in my gut it were going to end up killing me. / I got an ulcer off it.

MARY. Good. Good riddance I say.

BRIANA. I know why you brought me to live with you in 1981.

MARY. Not this again. I heard all this rubbish in court, Tina /

BRIANA. I'm not Tina, I'm Briana.

BRIANA *steps towards* MARY.

MARY (*shouts*). I don't care! Get out my house!

LEIGH *rushes up behind* BRIANA, *with the shard of glass from the broken picture in her hand,* JULIE *clocks it.*

JULIE (*screams*). Tina!

BRIANA *turns and sees* LEIGH *and the glass.*

BRIANA *grabs* LEIGH's *hand and they struggle.*

BRIANA *is stronger than* LEIGH *expected and she is overpowered.* LEIGH *kicks and struggles as* BRIANA *holds her down, screaming and screeching like a cat.* BRIANA *stabs the glass into* LEIGH's *hand.*

MARY. Oh my god, Leigh, get up – get off her! / Get up, Leigh

MARY *grabs at* LEIGH.

JULIE. / She's stabbed her in the hand!

LEIGH. She's stabbed me! Fuck, she's cut my fucking hand, Mary –

BRIANA *throws the glass clear, there is blood on both of them.*

The front door opens and BERNIE *enters.*

She's wearing a coat over her pyjamas.

Everyone is in a very small space.

BERNIE *grabs at* BRIANA.

BERNIE. Julie, help me, what you just standing there for?

JULIE. Mind there's glass on the floor.

LEIGH *gets out from* BRIANA*'s grip and runs through the open front door and into the night holding on to her bleeding hand.*

MARY. Where's she going?

(*Calls out.*) Leigh!

Oh my god she's run out the house!

BERNIE *tries to bundle* BRIANA *out of the house.*

BERNIE. Right. You. Out.

MARY. Julie, go after Leigh, she's got nothing on her feet –

BERNIE *has hold of* BRIANA *and is pushing her out the door.*

BRIANA *struggles and gets out of* BERNIE*'s grip and goes to run upstairs.*

BRIANA. I've done nothing wrong –

BERNIE. Julie, get her!

JULIE *tries to catch her and fails.*

BERNIE *grabs at* BRIANA *through the banister.*

BRIANA *runs up the stairs, into Mary's bedroom, and slams the door. She tries to push the dressing table back into its barricade position but it won't move.*

MARY. I can't believe *this*.

BERNIE. Right.

MARY. I've heard it all now.

BERNIE *pushes past* MARY.

BERNIE. Excuse me.

BERNIE *marches up the stairs and tries to open the door into* MARY*'s bedroom.*

BRIANA *leans her whole weight against it to keep it closed.*

BERNIE *can't open it.*

Tina. Will you get out my mother's house please.

BRIANA *doesn't answer, she is breathing heavily.*

MARY. Is she in my room?

BERNIE. Tina. Will you get out the house.

MARY. This is typical of her, your dad never wanted her y'know.

BERNIE. Open the door please. *Now*.

MARY. I said to him, she's your daughter, Ray. Her mother's in no state, who else is going to have her? I had to go and pick her up from Inglewood by myself. Two buses there two buses back. It took an hour and a half.

Her hair all matted, she'd never seen a brush.

(*Up the stairs.*) What is it you want from us, Tina?

They've written paedo on your dad's headstone because of you and you're still not happy!

BRIANA (*through the door*). No. They wrote paedo cos of what he *did* to me and you *knew* he was doing it.

Pause.

MARY. I can't hear a word she's saying.

Pause.

BERNIE. She's saying they wrote it because of what he did to her.

MARY. I don't need you chipping in like a bloody parrot thank you.

You'd think she'd be sick of her own voice by now.

MARY *sees* JULIE *standing in the hall.*

What you doing standing there for, get after Leigh before she bleeds to death and you've got her on your conscience as well as your son.

JULIE. You what? What's that supposed to mean?

MARY. I'm not arguing with ya, get after her, she's been stabbed! / She's running round with no shoes on!

JULIE. I've got nothing on my conscience. I did all I could for Michael. What you saying that for?

BERNIE. For Christ's sake, I'll go.

BERNIE *comes downstairs.*

Julie, do something useful, get upstairs.

BERNIE *leaves the house.*

JULIE *goes upstairs. She stands on the landing and knocks on the bedroom door.*

JULIE. Bri.

Upstairs in the bedroom, BRIANA *moves away from the door and sits on the bed.* BRIANA *is clutching her heart.*

JULIE *knocks again.*

Bri.

Silence.

MARY *stands alone in the hall downstairs.*

For a moment she seems disorientated, as if she's unsure where she is.

Blackout.

Out of the darkness, a shaft of light comes up in the box room.

JULIE *stands in the open doorway looking in.*

7.

LEIGH *is in the front room having her hand bandaged by* BERNIE.

There is a bowl of water and kitchen towel on the floor.

MARY *and* JULIE *are standing watching.*

ELLA *watches too, standing in the doorway in her coat holding a first-aid box.*

LEIGH *is holding her hand still while* BERNIE *bandages it, the bandage is already red with blood.*

LEIGH *is tutting and wincing.*

LEIGH. It's coming through the bandage –

BERNIE. I can see what's happening thank you /

MARY. That's not gonna last two minutes that, it's useless, where's that bandage from, Poundland?

JULIE. Pull it tight so it holds the two flaps of skin together /

BERNIE. I'll be cutting off the blood altogether if I pull it any tighter, she'll end up like that bloke with a hook.

LEIGH. It's hurting me!

BERNIE. Give over will ya, stop being a baby

MARY. Julie, get a towel for over your dad's chair.

JULIE. Dad's chair, what you talking about?

MARY. She's dripping blood all over.

JULIE. He's bloody dead! He's not gonna sit in it now, is he?

BERNIE. Pass us the other bandage, Ella.

ELLA. There's only like a stretchy one –

BERNIE (*to* LEIGH). Hold onto the end for me, I'm gonna wrap another bandage over the top.

LEIGH. It won't stop bleeding!

JULIE. Wrap it round tighter this time /

BERNIE. Alright, Florence! Why don't *you* do it?

MARY. I don't know why you won't call an ambulance get a proper paramedic to do it.

BERNIE. Don't be stupid.

MARY. What's stupid about that? It's their job!

She'll bleed to death at this rate.

BERNIE. Well, I wish she'd hurry up and do it, then I wouldn't have to listen to all you lot / telling us what to do.

LEIGH. Can you roll us a ciggy, Mary, there's baccy in my pocket.

BERNIE. Stay still. Give us the other bandage, Ella.

BRIANA *has come downstairs and is standing in the doorway beside* ELLA.

BRIANA *takes the bandage from* ELLA.

BRIANA. Give it here, I'll do it.

LEIGH. No way is she coming near me, she's a fucking psycho.

BRIANA. Get that bandage off, it's as good as useless like that.

JULIE. I told you.

LEIGH. She's not touching me.

BRIANA. I'm a trained first responder, I've got a certificate in it.

LEIGH. Oh yeah? Let's see it then.

BRIANA. I haven't got it on me, have I –

LEIGH *takes the bandage off herself.*

LEIGH. Eurgh, fuck's sake, this is *shit*.

BERNIE. It needs stitching but you won't go A and E!

BERNIE *takes the bloodstained bandage off* LEIGH.

LEIGH (*panicking*). I'm gonna bleed out!

BRIANA. Make a fist.

LEIGH. Yeah I will and I'll smash you in the face with it.

BRIANA. When the cut's down the centre of your palm like that, if you make a fist you're holding it closed yourself, you're helping yourself then, aren't you.

LEIGH *makes a fist.*

Right, now. I've got to bandage your hand closed in a fist like that.

LEIGH. Go on then, get on with it.

BRIANA *places the bandage on* LEIGH*'s hand and begins to wrap it round.*

BERNIE *watches for a moment then collects the bowl of water and paper towels together and takes them into the kitchen.*

Can't believe I'm letting you do this. I must be fucking mad.

BRIANA. Nice and still, good.

Everyone watches in silence while BRIANA *expertly bandages* LEIGH*'s hand held in a fist.*

MARY (*to* JULIE). She can go when she's done that.

JULIE. Alright, there's no need to be ignorant.

MARY. Oh so she breaks into my house at three o'clock in the morning and stabs an innocent girl and I'm ignorant?

LEIGH (*laugh*). Innocent girl that's funny!

BRIANA. I only wanted to talk to you.

MARY. You've got a strange way of going about it.

LEIGH. This bandage is good.

BRIANA. I told you, didn't I.

In the kitchen BERNIE *finds the open wine and pours it down the sink. She puts the kettle on.*

BERNIE (*shouts*). I've put the kettle on!

BRIANA *ties the bandage in place.*

BRIANA. I know why you came for me in 1981, Mary.

MARY. Oh here we go again.

BRIANA. You came for me because Julie was six and Bernie was three and you knew they were in danger. /

MARY. I'll get a restraining order out on you y'know.

BRIANA. And I was nine and you thought, well, she's messed up already, look at her, I'll get her back here and / then

MARY. Oh that's what I thought, was it? /

BRIANA. Yeh.

MARY. Psychic now are you an' all?

BRIANA. You thought, I'll throw Tina to the lions to save Julie and Bernie.

MARY. Did I?

BRIANA. Yeh.

BRIANA *finishes the bandage.*

But I forgive you for it, Mary.

I know you were trying to do right by them when you did wrong by me, but your little plan only half worked, didn't it, because Ray Dixon was even sicker in the head than you thought.

LEIGH. How am I supposed to have a smoke?

BRIANA. Use your other hand.

LEIGH. How am I gonna roll it with my hand like this?

BRIANA. Are you left or right handed?

LEIGH. What d'ya mean?

BRIANA. What hand do you normally write with?

LEIGH. What have I got to write for?

MARY. Don't think you can get your feet under the table by making friends with Leigh.

(*To* JULIE.) I want her *out*.

JULIE. This is more Briana's house than it is hers!

MARY. And you can get out an' all! You'd overstayed your welcome before you were born.

ELLA. Aww no, don't say that, Nana, that's horrible!

MARY. It's true! There's not a good bone in her body.

No wonder he's broke half of them.

ELLA. Nana!

BERNIE *comes out of the kitchen and into the doorway of the front room.*

BERNIE. What did she say?

JULIE *is looking at* MARY.

MARY. What's wrong with you?

She rolls her eyes and looks away.

JULIE. You know.

MARY. I know what? If you've got something to say, spit it out.

JULIE (*quiet*). When are you going to say sorry?

BERNIE. Jesus, Julie.

BRIANA. Go on, Julie /

MARY. Sorry for what? I've done nothing.

BERNIE. No, you're not doing this –

JULIE. Sorry for never doing anything about it.

BERNIE. Ella, go and put first-aid box back in the car please.

ELLA. Why?

BERNIE. Cos we're going in a minute. Mum, go back to bed.

JULIE. I can still remember the look on your face now.

MARY. You're drunk, Julie, you're always drunk. Your brain's that pickled, it'd be a miracle if you remembered anything right.

BERNIE. Do what I asked you please, Ella.

ELLA *leaves the room and takes the first-aid box out to the car.*

Say another word in front of Ella and I swear to god you'll be sorry.

JULIE. I can say what I like! What's she doing here anyway?

BERNIE. She had to drive me, didn't she? I've had four proseccos!

JULIE. I mean, what's she *here* for, why isn't she in Leeds?

BERNIE. What's that got to do with anything? / I mean it. Zip it.

BRIANA. / Julie

JULIE. Talk about blind eye.

BRIANA. Say what you need to say.

BERNIE. Tina, or whatever your fucking name is, I'm gonna tell you this once, you're not part of this family any more, you know nothing about it. I've put every drop of sweat into getting my daughter through exams and into university and over my dead body are you going rake this muck up and drag her under.

ELLA *comes back into the house.*

Who wants a tea? Leigh, you want a tea?

LEIGH. Yes please if it's not too much bother.

BERNIE. Mum, you want a tea?

MARY. I'd choke on it.

BRIANA. You'll never forgive me, and you'll never forgive Julie, will ya?

BERNIE. Are you still here?

BRIANA. Cos of how guilty we make you feel.

MARY. What have I got to feel guilty about? I did nothing!

BRIANA. I know! And doing nothing's a crime, Mary, especially when there's children involved. It's one of the worst crimes.

MARY (*to* LEIGH). See? Told ya, they all turn on me, don't they?

BERNIE. Ella, come and help me please.

BERNIE *leaves and goes into the kitchen.*

JULIE (*to* MARY). You opened the door and walked in –

BERNIE (*calling from the kitchen*). Ella!

ELLA *stays where she is.*

JULIE. – you said, 'why's this door closed?' and Dad said 'get out or I'll knock you out' –

LEIGH. Ha! You should of knocked *him* out, Mary!

JULIE. – and you just stood there staring and I was thinking why aren't you doing anything? Why aren't you saying anything to him?

MARY. I don't have to listen to this /

JULIE. You just closed the door, and went downstairs. It was the day before my fifteenth birthday.

MARY. Daughters are s'posed to take their mothers out on Mother's Day y'know, to a spa and a nice restaurant, when have any of you lot done that for me?

JULIE. What did you lie at Briana's trial for?

MARY. Oh right she's caught you in her web now, has she?

JULIE. You got off lightly. Your sentence wasn't long enough.

MARY. How *dare* you say that to me.

JULIE. You knew full well what he was.

BERNIE comes back into the doorway.

BERNIE. Ella. Come and help me, I've asked you that many times.

ELLA is staring at JULIE.

Ella?

Pause.

ELLA (*to* JULIE). Is Grandad, Michael's dad?

BERNIE gasps.

JULIE looks at BERNIE.

BERNIE. Oh my *god*, Ella!

ELLA turns to BRIANA.

ELLA. Is he?

BRIANA holds ELLA's eye but doesn't answer.

BERNIE. Of *course* he isn't! Tell her!

ELLA *stays looking at* BRIANA.

ELLA. Is he?

BERNIE. No! Of course not!

She looks at JULIE.

What have you been saying, look what you've started now!

ELLA. I've just realised. He is, isn't he?

BERNIE. Of course he isn't!

(*To* JULIE.) Tell her he isn't!

JULIE *doesn't answer.*

BERNIE *looks desperately at* MARY.

Mum. Tell her!

MARY *is hard-faced, closed.*

LEIGH *laughs nervously.*

BERNIE *holds onto the wall to steady herself, no one looks at her.*

Suddenly MARY *lunges forward and spits into* BRIANA's *face.*

BRIANA *holds her head up high. She nods.*

BERNIE *turns on* MARY.

Wait, did you *know*?

Have you *known* all this time?

BERNIE *turns to* JULIE.

Did you *know* she knew?

JULIE. She walked in and saw him, didn't she.

BERNIE *looks around the room in wild confusion.*

She turns back to MARY.

BERNIE. I thought –

I thought I was protecting *you* from –

But we've all just been protecting *him*.

Oh my *god*.

What's all this been *for*?

BERNIE *takes a packet of tissues from her handbag and drops it into* BRIANA's *lap.*

BRIANA. Thank you.

BRIANA *wipes the spit from her face.*

BERNIE *looks at* JULIE.

BERNIE. And you've waited till now?

In front of my Ella?

My *god*.

BERNIE *leaves the room and goes into the kitchen.*

LEIGH *makes eye contact with* BRIANA, *shrugs, makes a face, laughs.*

LEIGH. I've just thought, I'm gonna have to hold my tea in my other hand now.

Beat.

ELLA *gets up and follows* BERNIE *into the kitchen. She stands in the doorway.* BERNIE *turns her back to her.*

ELLA. Are you alright?

BERNIE. I never let you stay over here the night, did I?

Even when Stephen and Michael were stopping over.

I never *once* left you in the house with him.

ELLA. I know.

BERNIE. I want to go home.

ELLA. Now?

> BERNIE *waves* ELLA *away with her hand.*

BERNIE. I'm never stepping foot in this house again. Tell them. Tell them we're going home.

> ELLA *retreats, she hovers in the hall, in between both rooms.*

> *In the front room* JULIE *stands.*

MARY. I was up every night with that baby you had no interest in him.

JULIE. You had no interest in anyone except my dad, 'don't upset your dad, don't let that baby wake your dad'.

Why didn't you look after *me*?

MARY. I tried to, / you didn't want to know.

JULIE. How? *How?*

MARY. You've always been the same, Julie, you're impossible to help.

JULIE. What, when I was a child?

MARY. You wouldn't go back to school, you spent day and night behind the garages, / you were like a stray cat.

JULIE. Oh yeh, sorry about that.

MARY. You could have helped yourself, you should of kept out of his way /

JULIE. I. Was. A. Child.

MARY. Still, you could of defended yourself. *I* did!

LEIGH. Were you scared of him, Mary?

MARY. Yeh! Course I was.

LEIGH. Thought so.

MARY. He'd call me on the phone every forty minutes through the day. I had to pick up before three rings or he'd send one of his drivers round, check I was in the house.

Whatever I had to do, I had my forty minutes to get there, do it, get back. Shoes on, coats on, kids in the pram, out the door, food shop, lottery, I could never stop and talk.

My sister would say 'Mary, you're like a shadow.'

And he stopped me seeing my mother, even when she got cancer I couldn't go to her. He'd lock the door and take the key!

The way he *watched* me, I'd get my breathing trapped here in my chest, the way he *looked* at me.

He'd grab my face, squeeze it like this – wouldn't matter what I was doing, making him his dinner, he'd grab hold of my face, let the dinner ruin so I'd have to start again – If I looked at him it was wrong, if I didn't look at him it was wrong. I'd close my eyes and hope for the best. That would be wrong.

When my eczema flared up I'd get wrong for that as well, I couldn't please him!

BRIANA. He can't get us now though, can he?

Pause.

MARY. No.

And other times he was alright y'know.

JULIE *gets up and leaves the room.*

I can't even go back to bed, my bedroom's like a bomb's hit.

When JULIE *comes into the kitchen,* BERNIE *flicks on the kettle and puts a tea bag in a mug, wets a cloth and wipes the surfaces down.*

JULIE *clocks that the wine bottle is empty.*

BERNIE. Have you sorted somewhere to stay?

JULIE. No.

BERNIE. You can't stay here, can you?

JULIE. I know.

BERNIE. You can stop at ours if you want.

JULIE. Can I?

BERNIE. Just till you get yourself sorted, and you can't be watching television all night, Sanj has got to be up at five for work.

Pause.

JULIE. I might go home, Paul's calmed down.

He only gets bad when he's stressed.

He goes mad hanging round the house all day, he's going to see about some work on the new builds, they need electricians apparently.

Pause.

BERNIE. Don't go back to him, Julie.

JULIE. What if Michael comes looking for me and I'm not there?

JULIE looks as if she might break.

BERNIE wants to say something but she can't think what.

BERNIE puts her hand on the empty bottle, tipping it to see if there's a drop left in it.

BERNIE. Sorry – I poured it down –

JULIE recovers herself.

ELLA comes into the kitchen doorway.

ELLA (*to* JULIE). You alright?

BERNIE. Course she is, aren't you?

JULIE (*to* ELLA). How's your reading week going?

ELLA. Nana wants someone to sort her room for her, shall I go up with her?

BERNIE. Don't you dare – she's not having you running round after her.

BERNIE takes LEIGH*'s tea and goes into the front room.*

When BERNIE*'s left the room.*

ELLA. I saw Michael in Leeds, about a month ago.

JULIE. Did you, where? / What did he say?

ELLA. Outside Tesco on Boar Lane. He was asleep.

JULIE. Was he?

ELLA. At least I think it were him.

I didn't go up to him, I wasn't sure.

I was with my mates.

ELLA is tearful.

I wish I'd gone up to him now.

JULIE. Did he have a sleeping bag?

ELLA. I don't know, I think so. Most of them do.

JULIE. What do you mean, most of them? He's your cousin, y'know.

ELLA. I know he is, / I didn't mean that.

JULIE. Most of them? You're no better than him just cos you're with your uni mates.

ELLA. I know I'm not. I wish I'd gone up to him.

JULIE. A month ago? What use is that?

In the hall, BERNIE*'s phone rings, she answers.*

BERNIE. Hello love, have you just woken up?

–

I'm at a drag club with Ella and her uni mates.

Course I'm not I'm at my mother's.

Ella drove me.

BERNIE *opens the front door and steps outside.*

MARY *starts to walk upstairs,* ELLA *watches her.*

ELLA (*to* MARY). You going back to bed, are you?

MARY. My bedroom's like a bomb's hit it.

After a moment, MARY *goes upstairs,* ELLA *follows her up into her bedroom.*

JULIE *leaves the kitchen and stands in the doorway of the front room.*

JULIE (*to* BRIANA). Are you gonna put that settee back or what?

BRIANA. I know what 'Julie' means if you want me to tell ya.

JULIE. What?

BRIANA. Youthful, soft-haired, vivacious and a beautiful flower.

JULIE. Are you taking the piss?

BRIANA. No. That's what it means.

JULIE. Soft-haired? Does it?

JULIE *touches her hair.*

BRIANA. Look it up yourself if you don't believe me.

JULIE. What on?

BRIANA *doesn't answer.*

MARY *comes onto the landing and calls down.*

MARY. Julie! Get a dustpan and brush there's glass all over up here.

JULIE *goes into the kitchen.*

JULIE *finds the dustpan in the cupboard under the sink.*

Mary's bottle of Baileys is hidden in there. JULIE *pours herself a glass and drinks it.*

Upstairs in the bedroom ELLA *pulls back the duvet.*

MARY *sits on the bed.*

ELLA. You getting into bed, Nana?

MARY. I will in a minute.

ELLA. You alright?

MARY *stares ahead.*

Try and get some sleep, you can wake up bright and early. You'll feel better.

Pause.

Go for a walk, clear your head.

Get the bus to the cemetery.

MARY *shakes her head.*

MARY. I don't wanna go up there.

ELLA. I thought you said you did.

MARY. I can change my mind, can't I?

ELLA. Yeh, course you can.

MARY. I've got a mind of my own you know!

Pause.

Who am I now if I'm not his wife?

ELLA. –

JULIE *comes upstairs with the dustpan and brush.*

MARY. Take your time, I could have stepped on it by now and cut my foot.

JULIE *hands the dustpan to* ELLA *and turns to go back downstairs.*

ELLA. Tell her what you just said.

MARY. –

ELLA. About going up the cemetery.

MARY. You tell her.

ELLA. She's not going up there.

JULIE *does a face, 'so what?'*

You've changed your mind, haven't you, Nana?

MARY (*to* JULIE). Happy now?

JULIE. *Happy?*

MARY. It's what you want, isn't it?

JULIE. Don't do it for me, do it for yourself.

JULIE *goes back downstairs, walks past the front room and into the kitchen.*

ELLA *sweeps up the glass into the dustpan.*

MARY *lifts her feet up like a child, as* ELLA *sweeps up around her.*

When she's finished –

ELLA. You're a mother and a nana.

MARY *can't look at her.*

You said who are you – you're a mother. And a nana.

MARY. I don't know.

ELLA. You *are*.

MARY *doesn't look at her.*

ELLA *leaves the room and goes downstairs into the front room.*

BRIANA *is working on her laptop in the front room.*

ELLA *stands in the doorway, she tries not to cry.*

BRIANA *looks up.*

BRIANA. You crying?

ELLA. No.

BRIANA. What's the matter?

ELLA *cries*.

LEIGH. Aww, she's gonna make me cry now, I'm terrible,
I always cry when someone cries.

ELLA. I don't know why I'm crying though.

LEIGH. She's that pretty, she's pretty even when she's crying.

BRIANA. Have you left uni?

ELLA. I dunno, I've not been going in.

BRIANA. Why not?

LEIGH. I look dead ugly when I cry.

BRIANA. What have you stopped going in for?

ELLA. It's so fucked up.

BRIANA. What is?

ELLA. I'm sick of it I can't be doing with this, I'm so tired of
dealing with this.

BRIANA. With what?

ELLA. It's nothing just this tutor. / It's nothing.

BRIANA. What's he done?

ELLA. Nothing. It's nothing.

LEIGH. Do you want a smoke, you'll have to roll it, do you
want me to come outside with ya?

BRIANA. What is it?

ELLA. It isn't anything, just staring and making comments.
He only touched my neck, he only touched my chain – when
I pulled away he was like, is this a present from your
boyfriend?

LEIGH. Have you got a boyfriend then?

ELLA. No, not really.

LEIGH. Don't accept a drink off him.

BRIANA. What else?

ELLA. Nothing. Literally nothing!

BRIANA. Yes there is.

ELLA. He just makes these little comments like – I wanted an essay extension because Nana was in court, and I said I had family issues, and he said don't you mean boyfriend issues? I told him, no, I was just trying to get an extension and he kept on saying about a boyfriend, saying come on, Ellie, he calls me Ellie / you can tell me, Ellie

LEIGH (*big laugh*). I'd be like, is that my name? Is that my name though?

ELLA. Another time he was like, is that a birthmark? and he closed the door to his office. Which you're not supposed to do.

LEIGH. Were you wearing your hair up? They can get hold of it then, and jerk your head back.

ELLA. It's not like that, he's not going to do that. It's nothing.

Pause.

BRIANA. So you're gonna pack it in? Cos of him.

ELLA. Not cos of him –

BRIANA. Why then?

I thought you wanted to be a teacher.

ELLA. I dunno.

BRIANA. Have you made a formal complaint?

ELLA. Saying what?

BRIANA. All this you're saying now.

ELLA. Yeh, I did. I said about him to one of the other tutors,
this woman. And she was like, oh, yeah, ignore him,
everyone knows what he's like, he's gonna retire next year. /
I can't be doing with it, it's full of shit.

BRIANA. No. / No no.

BRIANA. She shouldn't be saying that to you, you can get her
done for that. You can get them both done. That's a violation
of the university's code of conduct.

ELLA. *What* is though?

BRIANA. Harassment. Intimidation. That's abuse of power.
Who's his boss?

ELLA. He acts like he's his own boss, I don't know.

LEIGH (*she lifts her hair off her face*). This is the hardest part
of your forehead here yeh, if you whack your head into the
middle of his face, keep your neck tense, smash his nose.
He's fucked.

BRIANA. There'll be an internal judicial process.

ELLA. He hasn't *done* anything though!

BRIANA. Stop saying he hasn't done anything you're telling
us, aren't you?

ELLA. It's just a feeling a wrong feeling you have to pretend
you don't notice and you know it *feels* wrong but not like
you could say it so it would *sound* wrong, it's just a feeling
do you know what I mean. You can't write it down on a
form. You can't knock him out for it or, report him for it. It's
like overreacting do you know what I mean you'd look like
you were mad, like he's just being friendly like you're stuck
up. Ugh I can't be bothered.

BRIANA. You can't be bothered what?

ELLA. Talking about it. It's just power over you, it's having all
the power, isn't it?

LEIGH (*sings*). / You got the power!

ELLA. He's got the power from being a tutor and he's got the power from being a man and he can stand close to me and look at me and say things that I can't say to him, and I'll pretend that I don't feel creeped out and avoid him or whatever and that's how it goes.

LEIGH. What's the heaviest weight that you can lift?

BRIANA. Right. What you gonna do about it then?

ELLA. Ignore him? Stop letting it bother me?

BRIANA. Stop letting it bother you.

Why's it you that's got to stop?

ELLA. Yeh I know.

BRIANA. Do you know what I mean?

ELLA. Yeh fuck's sake.

BRIANA. Stop letting it bother you, stop noticing it, stop mentioning it, stop minding about it, what's *he* gotta stop? Nothing.

LEIGH. Oi! Stop being a fucking perv, mate.

ELLA *looks at* LEIGH.

ELLA *looks at* BRIANA.

ELLA. I feel dead stupid saying all this to you. I know it's nothing /

BRIANA. / Shut up saying that.

ELLA. Compared to –

You were brave to say the stuff you said. In court and that.

BRIANA. You want kids?

ELLA. What?

BRIANA. Do you?

ELLA. I dunno yeh probably.

BRIANA. So when your daughter looks at you and asks –
'Why's the world's like this?'

ELLA. Okay I know what you're going to say.

BRIANA. 'Who gave them people permission to behave like
that to me?'

What will you say? 'Everyone, we all did.'

LEIGH. Not me fuck *off*.

BRIANA. 'No one could be bothered doing anything about it.
We were fed up talking about it.'

Nodding towards LEIGH.

She knows.

BERNIE *comes back into the hall.*

BERNIE. Ella, you alright to drive back?

ELLA. Yeh in a minute.

BERNIE *puts on her coat in the hall.*

Don't tell my mum.

BRIANA *starts to look up the university website on her
laptop.*

BRIANA. What's his name?

ELLA. Dr Mark Shaw.

LEIGH. I know him.

ELLA. Do you?

LEIGH. No.

ELLA *stands up.*

ELLA. Give us your number then.

BRIANA. That's it, listen to your Auntie Bri.

BRIANA *hands* ELLA *her card from a pocket in her laptop
case.*

ELLA. Shall I give you a text tomorrow?

BRIANA. Yeh, after nine.

ELLA. Also, I didn't tell you this but he went out with one of his students apparently like ten years ago and he's dead old like fifty and no one did anything about it.

BERNIE *calls from the hall*.

BERNIE. Who did?

ELLA. No one, I'm talking to Tina.

BRIANA. Briana.

ELLA. Briana.

BRIANA. We'll get this sorted.

ELLA. You're like Oprah you are.

ELLA *goes into the hall*. *She opens the front door.*

JULIE *comes out of the kitchen.*

BERNIE. You coming back with me and Ella?

JULIE. Alright.

BERNIE. Get your stuff then.

JULIE. I've not got anything.

BERNIE. Have you slept in those clothes? You're like Orphan Annie.

JULIE. My ears just popped. I've gone deaf in one ear.

ELLA. Dad's got conjunctivitis, he's blind in one eye.

BERNIE. You two'll make a right pair, won't you? C'mon.

JULIE *and* BERNIE *gather themselves to leave the house*.

ELLA. It's getting light.

LEIGH (*to* BRIANA). I'm gonna go college. I'm gonna do a certificate in bandages and stuff.

BRIANA. There's free courses online you know.

LEIGH. Is there?

Cos in A and E I'm always looking at the bits they use, they have to open a new packet, it's sterilised.

I could do that, I'd like to get a job there.

I tell them to show me, this nurse goes, you have to have a steady hand.

You have to be dead still so your heart gets slow and you don't get stressed out –

Sometimes I sit where they have the lights that go out when you don't move.

Sometimes a toilet in a hotel.

They have it in a waiting room as well. The ones in a train station.

If you stay really still then the lights go off and you get to see what the room looks like when you're not in the room.

Afterwards you see all the people – the way they rush. People working in a shop. People with a dog.

Because everybody's good at something.

I was good at science and that – I got the top mark once, what was it, A. Yeah like maths and something else you had to set fire to it, it went different colours, I was the top mark.

They kept saying about I had nits.

JULIE *pokes her head round the door.*

JULIE. See ya. Wouldn't wanna be ya!

BRIANA *ignores her.*

You staying here, are you?

BRIANA. Just while I do this.

JULIE. Using the wifi.

BRIANA. Yeh.

JULIE. I'm gonna stop at Bernie's.

BRIANA. Okay.

JULIE stands up straight and salutes.

JULIE. Tina, look, straight back.

BRIANA looks at her.

BRIANA. Yeh. Take care of yourself.

JULIE. Can't believe that, what was it, a beautiful flower?

BRIANA goes back to her laptop.

JULIE goes out into the hall.

LEIGH closes her eyes in the chair.

JULIE and BERNIE and ELLA leave the house.

Silence.

Birdsong.

MARY gets out of bed and comes downstairs.

MARY comes into the doorway of the front room.

MARY. Leigh.

Leigh.

BRIANA. She's asleep.

MARY stays in the doorway.

A stranger in her own house.

Don't worry I'll put the room back how it was, before I go.

MARY. It's okay. Leave it.

MARY goes into the kitchen and gets a bucket and a stiff brush out from under the sink.

MARY fills the bucket with water from the tap.

MARY *comes into the front room and kneels on the floor
next to the large stain on the carpet.*

She starts to scrub the stain.

She puts her whole weight into it.

She scrubs and scrubs.

MARY *stops to rest for a few seconds.*

BRIANA *stands.*

I'll do it.

MARY *scrubs some more.*

BRIANA *watches her.*

Lights slowly fade to black.

The End.

CLE/N
BRE\K

WHO WE ARE

Clean Break is a women's theatre company established in 1979 by two women at HMP Askham Grange in Yorkshire. For over forty years we have used theatre to transform the lives of women with criminal justice experience, to challenge preconceptions and inspire new narratives.

WHAT WE DO

Our award-winning theatre productions share the often-hidden stories of women and criminalisation. We are proud to have co-produced our new plays with dozens of UK theatres, including the Royal Court Theatre, Donmar Warehouse, Manchester Royal Exchange, Birmingham Rep, Theatr Clwyd, the Royal Shakespeare Company, Soho Theatre, Sheffield Theatres, and the Bush Theatre.

We have engaged with thousands of women on the fringes or with experience of the criminal justice system (our Members) from our women-only building in Kentish Town; a safe space where creativity happens, and transformation becomes possible. The programme's success has grown generations of highly skilled and confident women, 70% of whom currently progress to further studies, employment, or longer-term volunteering.

'This really is a lifeline helping me to create a new world, a new life for me.' **Clean Break Member**

Clean Break has been fortunate to work with many extraordinary writers and creatives. Our commissioning process offers a unique exchange between artists, our Members and women in prison.

'As a young female playwright, lots of the texts I was picking up were commissioned by Clean Break. And it wasn't about women walking into places and shooting everybody, it wasn't highly glamorised. I really felt drawn to the quiet craft, the kindness.' **Alice Birch on writing for Clean Break, 2019**

SUPPORT US

We can't do what we do without you. If you want to help transform women's lives, please visit our website, www.cleanbreak.org.uk/support

CLEAN BREAK STAFF

CLEAN BREAK DEVELOPMENT COMMITTEE

Tracey Abayeta
Honour Bayes
Elise Brown
Sarah Jane Dent
Sophie Fiori
Sharon Heyman
Catherine Hinwood
Alison Jefferis [Chair]
Sarah Jeffs
Gillian Jones
Rebecca Urang

Clean Break would like to acknowledge the generosity of all its funders and supporters.

KEEP IN TOUCH

Be first in the know for all Clean Break's news by signing up to our newsletter via our website, or follow us on our social media channels:

Twitter: @CleanBrk
Facebook: /cleanbreak
Instagram: @CleanBrk

Clean Break
2 Patshull Road
London
NW5 2LB
020 7482 8600

general@cleanbreak.org.uk
www.cleanbreak.org.uk

Registered company number 2690758
Registered charity number 1017560

www.nickhernbooks.co.uk

facebook.com/nickhernbooks

twitter.com/nickhernbooks